STAR WARS®

EPISODE I

HEROES AND VILLAINS COLORING BOOK

written by Michelle Knudsen
illustrated by Jesus Redondo

Random House 🏠 New York
LucasBooks

ISBN: 0-375-80021-2

www.randomhouse.com/kids
www.starwars.com

Printed in the United States of America 10 9 8 7 6 5 4 3 2 1

Anakin Skywalker

Kitster and Amee are two of Anakin's friends.

Kitster is Anakin's best friend.

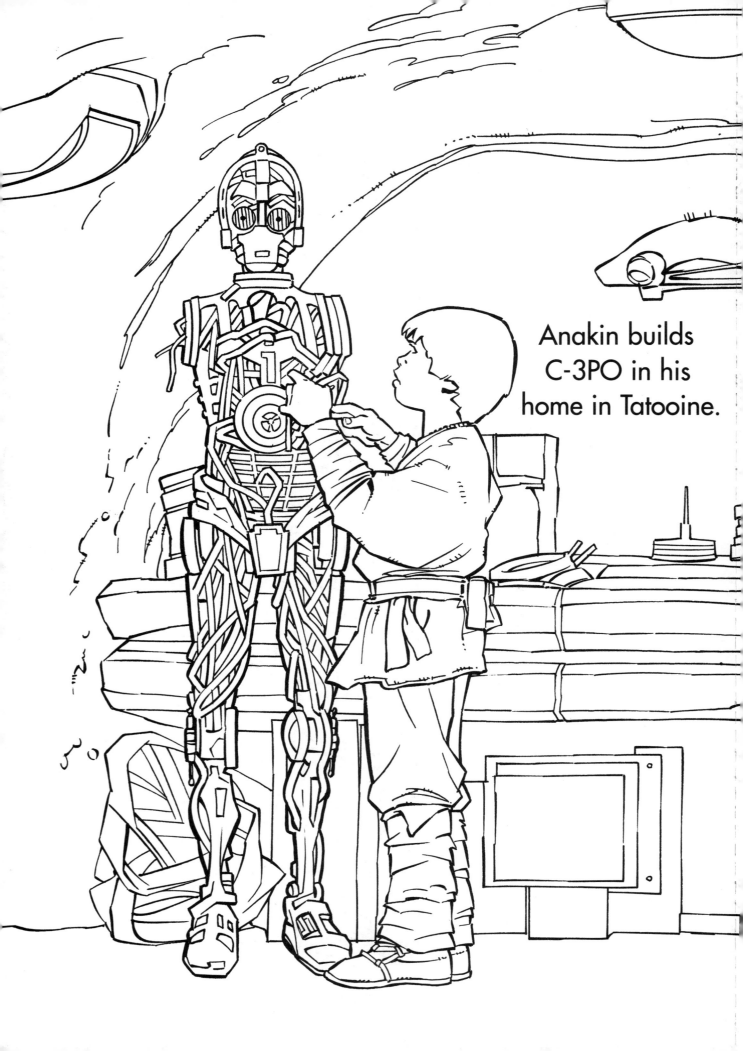

Anakin builds
C-3PO in his
home in Tatooine.

Anakin is
also building
his own Podracer.

Jira runs a fruit stand
near Anakin's home.

Anakin is
always kind to Jira.

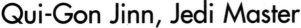

Qui-Gon Jinn, Jedi Master

Obi-Wan Kenobi,
Jedi apprentice

Qui-Gon is teaching Obi-Wan how to be a Jedi Knight.

Obi-Wan
doesn't always
agree with his Master.

Queen Amidala,
ruler of Naboo

The Queen rules from her palace in Theed, Naboo's capital city.

Queen Amidala has clothing
for every occasion.

Some of the Queen's
handmaidens

Padmé Naberrie is a
very special handmaiden.

Queen Amidala
shares an important secret with Padmé.

Captain Panaka,
Queen Amidala's
protector

Royal Security Forces of Naboo

Sio Bibble,
Governor of Naboo

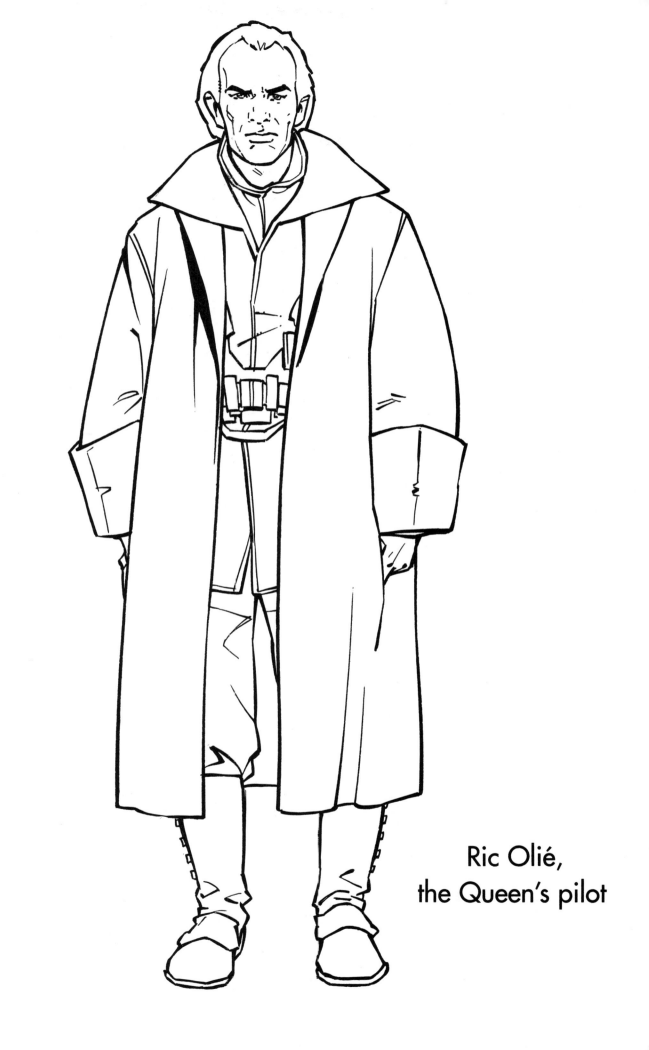

Ric Olié,
the Queen's pilot

Ric Olié skillfully pilots the Queen's ship
past the Trade Federation blockade.

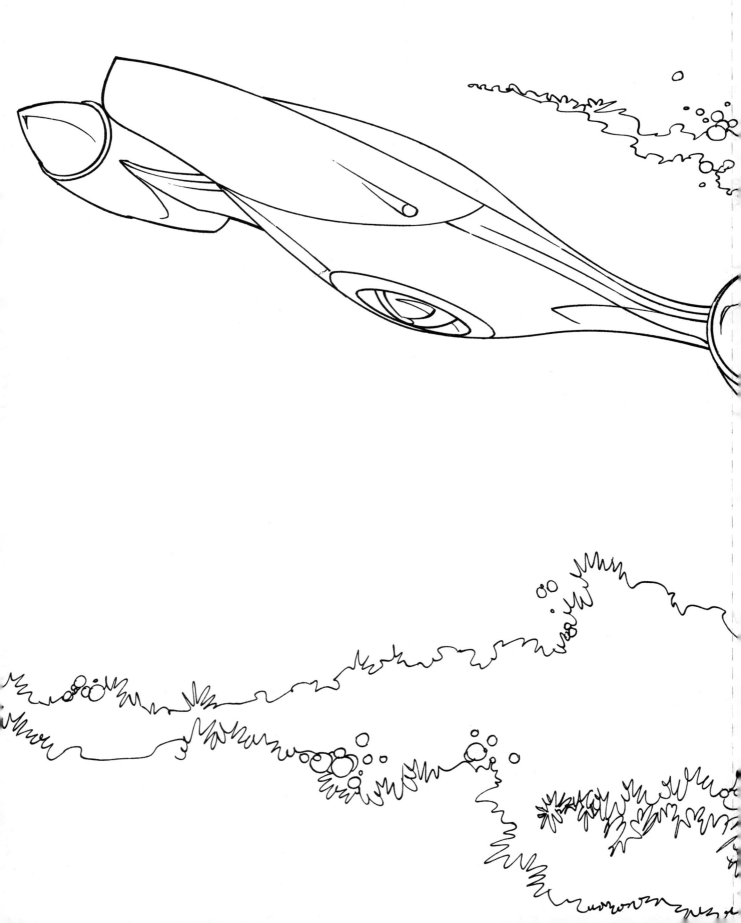

Boss Nass,
leader of Otoh Gunga

Jar Jar Binks,
exile from Otoh Gunga

Jar Jar teams up with Qui-Gon in the swamps of Naboo.

Gungan soldiers
ride kaadu into battle.

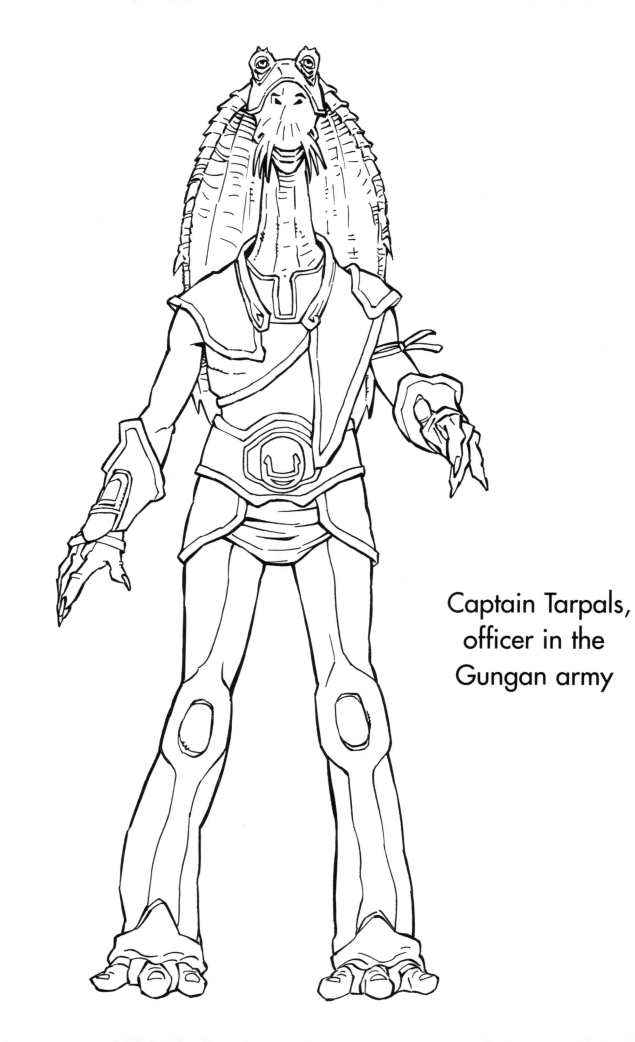

Captain Tarpals,
officer in the
Gungan army

Supreme Chancellor
Valorum is the leader
of the Republic Senate.

Mace Windu, senior Jedi

Ki-Adi-Mundi
of the Jedi Council

Jedi Master Yoda

Adi Gallia

Eeth Koth

Depa Billaba

Yarael Poof

Qui-Gon asks the Council
to test Anakin's Jedi abilities.

Darth Sidious,
Dark Lord of the Sith

Darth Maul is
Darth Sidious's apprentice.

The Sith Lords are powerful enemies of the Jedi.

Darth Sidious forms an alliance with the Trade Federation.

He sends Darth Maul to stop the meddling Jedi Knights.

Qui-Gon fights to protect the Queen!

Qui-Gon and Obi-Wan find that
Darth Maul is a dangerous foe!

Nute Gunray,
Neimoidian Trade
Federation Viceroy and
ally of Darth Sidious

Rune Haako,
member of the
Trade Federation and
ally of Darth Sidious

Jabba the Hutt, member
of the infamous Tatooine crime family

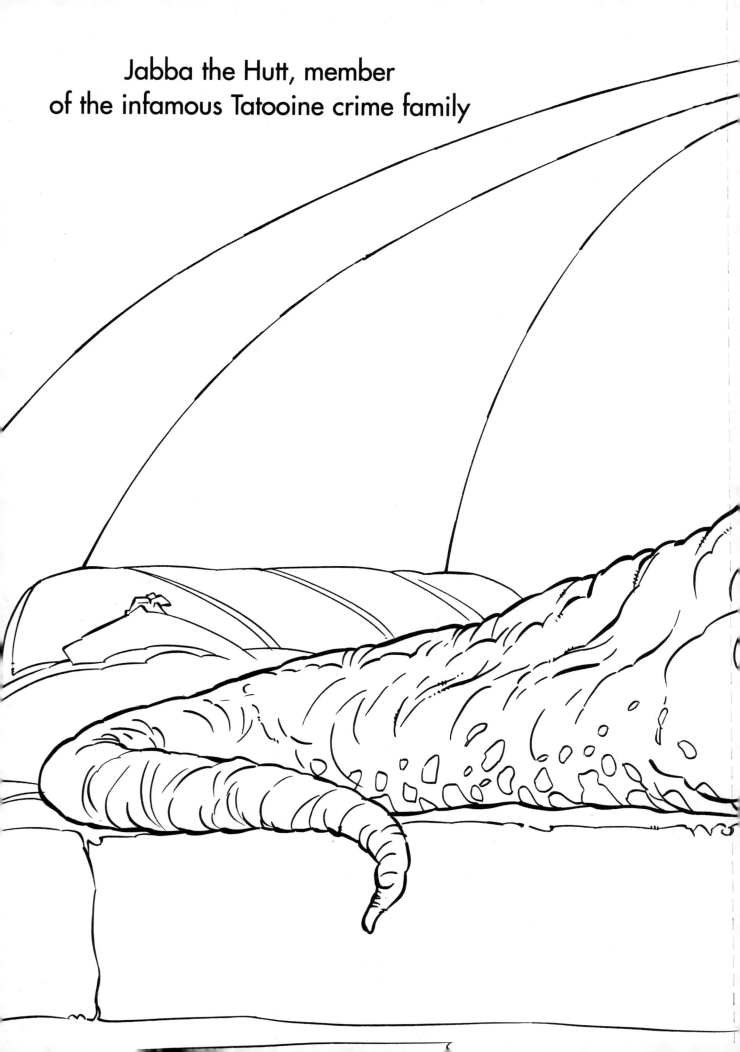

Wald, a troublemaker
who picks on Anakin

Qui-Gon helps Anakin
see that fighting won't
solve this problem.

Watto, junk shop owner

Anakin works
in Watto's junk shop.

Watto is not the kindest of masters.

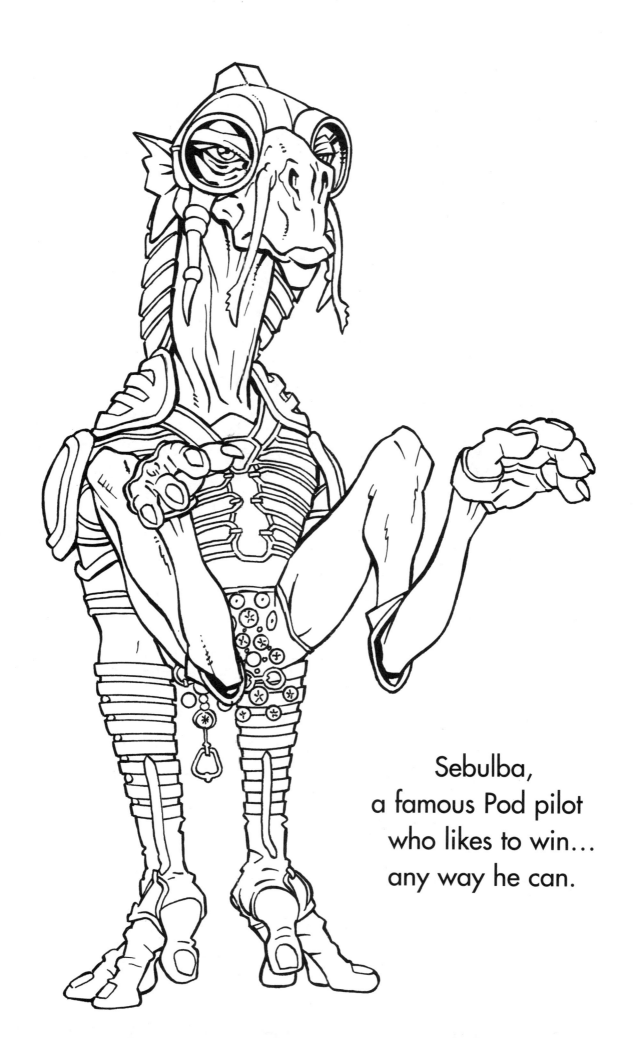

Sebulba,
a famous Pod pilot
who likes to win…
any way he can.

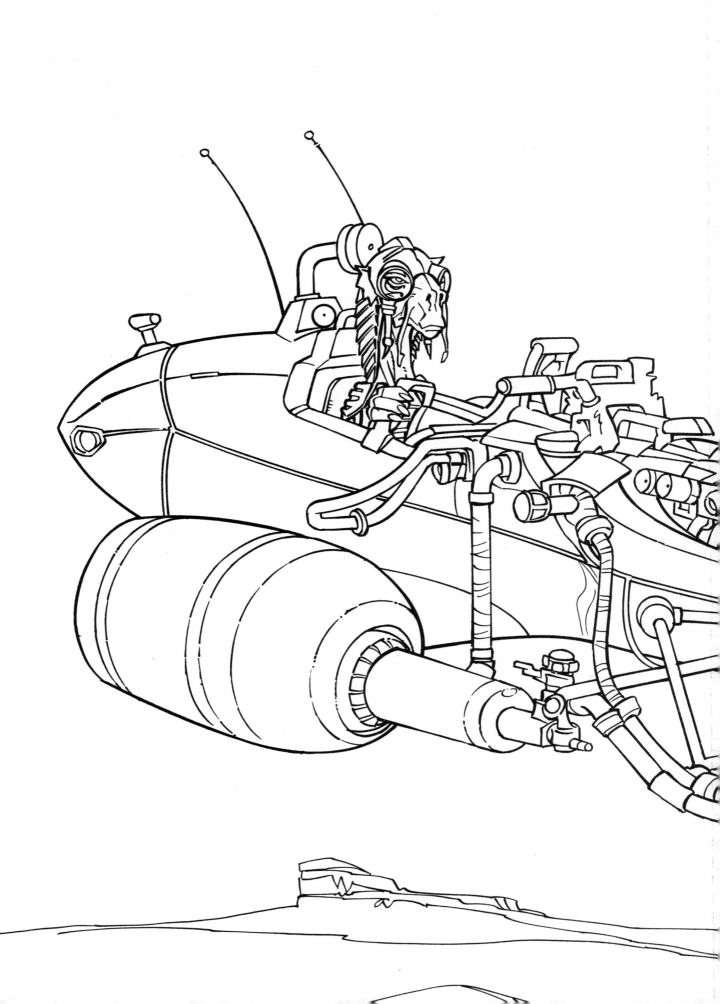

Sebulba wants to beat Anakin in the Podrace.

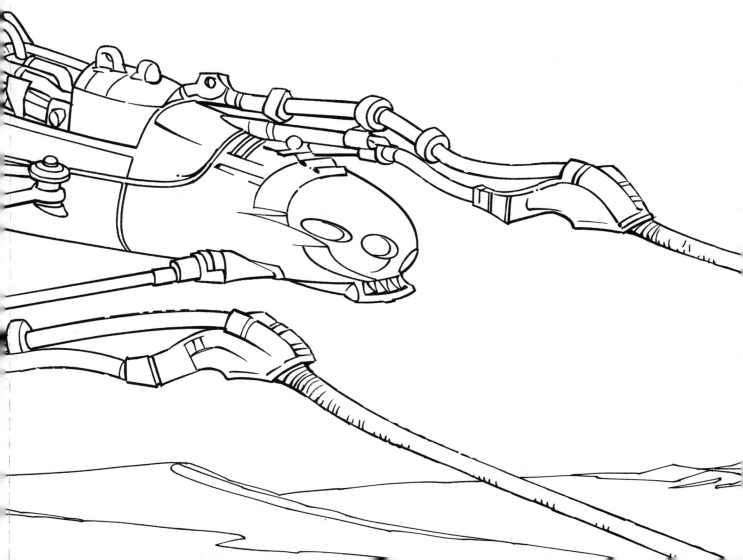

Who is firing at the Podracers?

Senator Palpatine
of Naboo

Queen Amidala looks
to Senator Palpatine
for guidance.

The Queen has many
important decisions to make.

There are lots of villains in the galaxy.

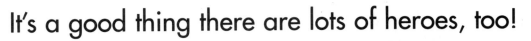
It's a good thing there are lots of heroes, too!